Dance: A Spiritual Affair

CREATIVE SPIRIT SERIES
BOOK ONE

DONNA GODDARD

Copyright © 2020 (1st edition), 2023 (2nd edition) by Donna Goddard

All rights reserved. No part of this book may be reproduced in any form or by any electronic or mechanical means, including information storage and retrieval systems, without written permission from the author, except for the use of brief quotations in a book review.

Cover design by Donna Goddard

Contents

Introduction — v

PART ONE
DANCING FLAME

1. The Flame Ignites — 3
2. Change and Comfort — 5
3. Following Interests as an Adult — 7
4. Balance — 11
5. Neither Beginning nor End — 14
6. Being in Our Body — 18
7. Injury as Teacher — 21
8. Interior and Exterior Worlds — 24
9. Still and Sacred — 27
10. Energy Centres — 31
11. Ballroom and Latin — 35
12. Fulfilling Our Potential — 40
13. Pas De Deux — 47
14. Demand and Supply — 53
15. The Stalls of Life — 56

PART TWO
STORIES IN STORIES

16. Dance Thread — 63
17. Waldmeer Series — 64
    A Spiritual Fiction Series
18. Nanima Series — 80
    Spiritual Fiction

PART THREE
DANCER BIOGRAPHIES

19. The Winged Life — 93
20. Ruth St. Denis — 94
21. Veloz and Yolanda — 99
22. Ginger Rogers — 103

PART FOUR
POETRY ABOUT DANCE

23. Perfect Mismatch — 109
24. Heart of Existence — 111
25. Dissolve — 112
26. Still Point — 114
27. Melded — 115
28. Grand Old Man — 116
29. Wandering Words — 118
30. Burn Up — 119

Creative Spirit Series — 121
About the Author — 123
Also by Donna Goddard — 125

Introduction

Dancing is an innately spiritual affair. It reaches beyond words to the essence of beauty. Its height is Divinity. Its depth is humanity. It is the ever-moving balance between independence and intimacy. All the while, it reaches into the great Beyond. This book is written from the perspective of an adult dance student. However, it delves into the physical, emotional, and spiritual significance of dance across the board.

PART ONE
Dancing Flame

CHAPTER 1
The Flame Ignites

I had resigned myself to the idea that dancing, for me, would be an unfulfilled yearning. In my mid-twenties, I told myself I was too old for dancing and should transfer all such longings into a more suitable outlet. The dancing flame was buried, and I took up the violin. Playing the violin was enjoyable enough, but I wasn't a musician. I was a dancer.

In my early thirties, I went back to university to do a Diploma of Education so that I would be able to work as a teacher. I thought teaching would fit in with raising young children on my own. One of the short options in the diploma was dance. As soon as I began the dance option, the dancing flame ignited. It came alive. It was given oxygen, and it started to breathe with a great gust of enthusiasm and relief. I was amazed because I no longer knew it was there and certainly did not know the intensity with which it waited for air. How wonderful it felt. How deeply it touched me. I felt something in me that was different to all the other parts of me, and it felt uniquely beautiful and satisfying. Alas, the dance option was over too quickly, and I returned to the academic task at hand.

When the Diploma of Education was completed, life carried on. One day, I asked myself if I needed to do something different to improve the quality of my life. Naturally, the dancing flame leapt at the opportunity as it had only been a short time ago that it felt its first breath in nearly a decade.

"Don't be ridiculous. You can't take up dancing now," warned my rational mind. "You are a responsible mother of two young children. Grown-up women don't dance."

"Oh, be quiet," my free mind said in reply. "I could be dead in a year. Then what would it matter?"

I did not die. I did take up dancing—in the form of ice skating. I skated for thirteen years with great enjoyment. Like a friend who was lost and then refound, the bond is protected at all costs. I later transferred to ballroom dancing, which I loved even more.

Dancing has helped me to feel connected to myself and life. It fulfils an inner drive that has remained with me since I was a young child with a treasured picture of beautiful ballet couple Margot Fonteyn and Rudolph Nureyev. I didn't know who they were, but they were fascinating and lovely. We are no one else. We are ourselves. We must be that, with no regrets, if we wish to be happy. If we keep going forward, following our natural, intuitive, and sincere path, everything will tend to align with our good intention.

CHAPTER 2
Change and Comfort

Significant change (such as my transfer from ice skating to ballroom dancing) often involves a disconcerting crossover stage, a period of choppy sailing when we can't quite tell what's going on, if we are doing something wrong, or if the situation is now wrong for us. I distinctly remember the stinging discomfort of my last ice skating class.

After thirteen years of adult ice skating, it wasn't working anymore. At that point, there was only one ice rink in my city and a small pool of teachers available (no one I felt was right for me). However, after all the years of fun, challenge, friendship, drama, and love, we are usually most reluctant to throw the towel in. The discomfort with the situation continued to escalate until one Wednesday morning in my "Ladies Class", which I had greatly enjoyed for most of those years, I felt utterly miserable. So bad, so depressed, that all I could do was skate around the rink lifelessly, trying not to cry. The feeling forced the issue. At the end of the class, I told myself that I couldn't continue to skate if it made me feel so terrible. I had tried everything to make it work, but it no longer was and no longer could. It was over, and I had to face it. I only faced it because of the escalating pain of not facing it.

However, as soon as I admitted to myself that it was over, I got a brilliant idea. Join the ballroom dancing world. Unlike the sad state of ice skating, which had deteriorated to one rundown rink and hardly any teachers, there were many ballroom dance studios and teachers. The studios were warm (and maybe the teachers were too), and you didn't fall over and slide over concrete-like ice, which was a good idea at the age I was by then (forty-five). At the end of the week, I tried a local dance studio. Being new, it was a little awkward, but I liked it. Within a few weeks, I felt right at home and thus began an absorbing and enthralling journey of many years and still counting.

CHAPTER 3
Following Interests as an Adult

It is wonderful when people take up something as an adult that they always wanted to do but, for one reason or another, couldn't previously do. As a child, they may not have had the opportunity to follow an interest (maybe because their family was busy surviving life). The activity may be taken up as soon as we become young adults and start making decisions about our life direction and where we want to spend our time and money. Sometimes, it can happen much later in life when the demands of children, mate, and work are in a different category of required input.

Here are a few guidelines for those who enter dancing as an adult.

1. *We are our bodies before we are a dancer.* Have a serious look at the state of your body, and gradually and deliberately turn it into a healthy and strong one. Undoubtedly, one can do a great deal right into very senior years if one puts one's mind to it consistently. Along the way to improving the general state of our body, we can also specifically turn it into a dancer's body (as much as possible).
2. *Get your weight right.* Look at what you eat. If it is not healthy and in harmony with your body type, then change it. If that involves some mental work (which it usually does), then do the work. Chinese medicine and Ayurvedic (Indian) medicine are valuable resources on the different body types and the food required for each.
3. Look at your body's *flexibility, fitness, and strength* before assessing it as a dancer's body. Learn how to improve your body's wellness as a complete entity. This will probably involve doing out-of-dance sessions in disciplines such as yoga, Pilates, or whatever interests you and improves your physical capabilities. You won't notice the work if you enjoy the activity. For my entire adult life, I have walked every day, usually several times a day. Sometimes, it has been with little children, frequently with dogs. Regardless, I love to walk. It clears my mind. Walking in nature is best. It is thinking time and also stillness time. Even if walking had no beneficial effects on the body, I would still do it. If we can find physical activities that we

sincerely enjoy, it will effortlessly benefit our body.
4. *Work on your injuries and illnesses.* Most bodies accumulate various injuries and illnesses. Do something about yours. Don't just ignore them. Find out how they got there and how you can eliminate them. Look into whatever professions improve your knowledge and the state of your well-being, such as Western and Eastern medicine, physiotherapy, chiropathy, naturopathy, acupuncture, massage, shiatsu, and energy healing. Each has a wealth of information and wisdom to pass on. Some will be precisely what you need. It can be a bit of an ongoing process because it seems no sooner do we master one body problem than another decides to make an appearance!
5. While doing all of the above, also have your dance lessons. *Go to the best people available to you.* Go to teachers and classes that you genuinely enjoy. If you are no longer learning what you need or enjoying the process, go somewhere else. After all, your number one reason for dancing is enjoyment.
6. *Don't compete or compare* with young serious dancers or older professional dancers. Their main path in life has been dance. Some have been on it for a long time. They dance every day. Let them be them, and we'll be us. Having said that, most people expect way too little of themselves. The body, mind, and spirit can do much more, at any age, than most people give it credit for. We can keep expanding our

expectations while not being sabotaged by unrealistic goals or jealous competitiveness. We can sincerely be grateful that everyone in the dance world is present and bringing what they have to give. Our happiness is assisted not by the demise of another person but rather by the authentic fulfilment of each one's potential. Such an attitude saves us many problems and worries. It also protects us from the competitive nature of others. The more our ego is present, the more material an enemy has to grab onto and manipulate. The more our attention is on achieving what is good for everyone, the more an enemy will struggle to pull us down. Somehow, things will ultimately keep working in our favour.

CHAPTER 4
Balance

It is wise to do our best in every area of life to improve our well-being and happiness. If we feel that our life is not balanced, it is a good idea to take stock of the energy we put into the various aspects of our being.

- Are we physically well?
- Do we need more exercise?
- Do we respect our body by giving it what it needs to eat?
- Are we physically ill in some way? Ignoring one's physical problems is hardly a recipe for health.
- Are we mentally stressed?
- Do we take enough time each day, week, and year to relax and relieve our nervous system?
- Do we organise and prioritise our lives so we do not suffer from constant nervous exertion? Many of our time problems are really priority issues.

- Do we challenge our mental capacities? Do we read and think about issues of importance to us?
- Do we further our knowledge, understanding, and, if appropriate, qualifications in our fields of interest?
- Do we monitor our emotions so they do not lead us on a merry chase?
- Do we demonstrate gratitude for life by doing things we love to do and furthering the talents God has given us?
- Do we consistently, patiently, unselfishly, and sincerely practise love and forgiveness?
- Do we practise these same virtues towards ourselves?

Sometimes, people say they are very spiritual, but one only has to take a cursory look at their lives to see how much truth is in that.

- Are they lazy about their health, blatantly ignoring their bodies that are calling out for attention?
- Do they try to calm and reorient out-of-control emotions such as blame and self-pity?
- Are they treated with respect by intelligent people?
- Do they hold grudges that they refuse to acknowledge?
- Do they radiate unpleasantness and selfishness to those around them while proclaiming their great spiritual interest?

The state of our body, mind, and heart speaks volumes about where our true interests lie. Let those interests be kind, intelligent, and dedicated to the Good.

CHAPTER 5
Neither Beginning nor End

AGEING

Most people age much earlier than necessary. By thirty, many are already old in themselves. By forty, most have lost the spark of life. By fifty, a lot of people seem senior. All of this is entirely preventable and, to a large extent, reversible.

Ageing happens at all levels of our being, but the most obvious is the body. *Use it or lose it.* One of the reasons I dance, apart from my love of it, is that my teachers (who are generally much younger than me) push me to keep using my body in ways that I otherwise wouldn't. In large dance classes, I will often intentionally stand next to the twenty-year-old exuberant dancers as their energy (of which they have masses to spare) helps me. This is why young children and senior citizens go together beautifully. The fresh life of children ignites the elderly, and the children are calmed down by their older relatives' more low-key energy.

Of course, you will be fighting a losing battle if you

only exercise your body and not your mind and spirit. When you use them all, they will gladly and efficiently work together. Although we cannot stop the march of time on our use-by-stamped bodies, we can have the blessings of a well-functioning and alive body, an active and bright mind, and a loving and expressive soul.

LATECOMER TO THE PARTY

Socrates began dancing at age seventy because he felt he had "neglected something important" within himself. He did not limit himself but felt the joy of discovery in later years. Master teacher and choreographer Bert Balladine told his students in a 1987 workshop, "A woman doesn't have anything to dance about until she's over thirty-five!" Thirty-five is considered the senior end for dancers, particularly back then. One of the directors of the Australian Ballet said, "By the time you are old enough to understand ballet, you are too old to do it." Ballet, one of the most challenging dance forms, usually requires the athleticism of youth, but the depth of ballet's stories is often lost on young dancers.

If you are an older dancer (and you can be old by professional standards even when you are still young), do not see yourself as a regrettable latecomer to the party who has somehow missed out on all the good stuff. Consider that dance has found you at exactly the right time of your life for you to get maximal physical, social, and spiritual benefit from it.

AUTHENTICITY AND ALLEY CATS

My dance class had a guest teacher, a renowned local flamenco dancer with thirty years of performance experience. Although young dancers are admired for their speed and agility in flamenco, they are not considered to have the emotional maturity to convey *duende* or soul adequately. The most respected flamenco dancers are the older dancers who long ago mastered their technique and now perhaps do less with their body but more with their soul.

Young dancers have beautiful, strong, flexible, and resilient bodies. And they have the fire of hope in their heart. However, the fire can be a bit feral, like a young alley cat. It can go everywhere, in all directions, willy-nilly. It can turn all claws and spit or get nervous and run away. It pretends things that aren't true and is afraid of showing what is true.

The older cat bides their time. They have patience. They pull the fire inside and let it smoulder. They don't waste energy on fights not worth the battle or where the casualties would be greater than the goal. They own their failures like scars saying it would be wise to take them seriously. They are not ashamed of their loves. They value their spirit and let it grow. It's in the eyes. The body may move less, but it has presence and power of a different sort. It is authentic.

FRESH MINDSET

With the right mindset, we can have highly productive lives at any age. A youthful spirit attracts vibrant people into its circle of influence. We are not young and we are not old. The Infinite neither begins nor does it end. This is the inherent nature of our life force. To free ourselves from the limitations of age is to encompass a journey full of adventure, growth, success, fulfilment, and surprising achievements. If we do not limit ourselves with notions of age, we will find that life will oblige by also disregarding many of the limitations of age. We will be attractive to others because, far from being a burden, we will have something worthwhile and valuable to offer all through the blossoming years.

CHAPTER 6
Being in Our Body

FILING FOR DIVORCE

Not infrequently, people say after an illness, "I didn't see that coming." Yet, their body was probably screaming at them to listen. The warning signs can be ignored through denial, fear, ignorance, and laziness. People are generally unaware of the conversation their body is constantly having with them. They become focused on career, family, and mortgage. The years pass by with only a token look at the state of the body. Sometimes, it is just too much effort, and knowing where to begin can seem overwhelming. Stress, neglect, lack of awareness, and concentrating on more mental pursuits can pull us away from our relationship with our body. Like a neglected partner, the body can be forgotten. It will be relied on for its loyalty but barely given the time of day. Naturally, the body (and the partner) will start complaining and may eventually file for divorce with ruinous consequences.

BODY WISDOM

Our body is important. It's the first gift God gives us. We are meant to take care of it the entire time we have it. We are meant to be grateful for it, use it, enjoy it, and learn from it. At the same time, we are not meant to obsess over it, be vain, be a hypochondriac, or be a pleasure-seeker at other people's expense. A body has its own wisdom. It knows things independently of the mind. It knows its weakest parts. It knows the places we have neglected. It knows the parts we have never even met.

Talking to our body can be a little confronting at first. It can be rather direct. If we don't listen, it can slam us with some noisy physical condition or pain, so we have to pay attention. It is not just physical exercise that the body needs. We must learn how to balance and harmonise all its different aspects. In yoga, the conscious, intelligent attention to muscles, organs, and energy centres will do just that. Focusing on the whole rhythm and flow of our being brings far more than exercise alone can ever do.

YOGA

Yoga is old—very old. That is why it knows all about us. It knows that every part of our body affects every other part. It is holistic, working on the body, mind, and spirit. We cannot shut off one part of our being without suffering the consequences. Yoga first deconstructs the body and then forms it anew. Leave your competitiveness at the yoga studio door. Take it off with your shoes. It has no place within the sanctioned walls of the yoga studio and will only lead to injury. Breathe in the incense and take in the centuries of yogic knowledge, which strives to form you into a healthy and life-filled being. Be humble. Acknowledge how you are not well, strong, supple, and calm. Be brave. Yoga is your friend and will help you become the beautiful, grounded being waiting for you. An aware person can apply the same approach to any discipline. Dancing, if you let it, will also unmake you before it remakes you anew.

CHAPTER 7
Injury as Teacher

ALL LEVELS

Naturally, injuries should be assessed on a physical level by people who are qualified to do so. However, there is, above and beyond the physical, a vital connection between injuries and our mental and energetic state of being. That connection is generally neither understood nor made use of for recovery purposes. Injuries need to be approached from the various levels of our being—physical, mental, emotional, and spiritual.

GOOD SORE

Let's begin with the teaching role of injuries on a physical level. Injuries are not simply negative things (ranging from annoying to life-altering) that must be eliminated. They are teaching mechanisms. For example, some years ago, when I altered my dancing regime from two lessons a week and no practice to a much more rigorous routine of lessons, classes, and lots of practice, I was obviously asking a great deal more of my body, which was far from young. Nevertheless, I felt confident that it would cope. It did cope. It coped much better than I thought it would. But when we up the ante for our body, it is going to complain. During that first year of my dramatic dancing increase, my body was sore, in one way or another, every single day. It was mostly *a good sore*— a natural reaction to being asked to wake up and move more.

BAD SORE

Additionally, there was a component of pain that was *injury-based*. That component extended much longer than one year. Every time I concentrated on improving my skill level in one particular area of my body, I would end up injuring it. It wasn't from overuse, although there may have been an element of that. It was mostly that I was moving that part incorrectly (or not correctly enough) for the number of repetitions I was doing.

At one stage, it was my lower back. I learned how to use my core muscles more effectively, which fixed that problem. Then, I went through a stage of increasing the engagement of my upper back muscles. You guessed it. I developed pain in my upper back and shoulders and had to improve the way I was moving so that I wasn't creating so much tension.

As my dancing focus moved to various parts of my body, so did the injuries. The point of this example is not to recommend an assorted array of moving injuries. It is to explain that each injury forced me to correct my technique and improve my ability and understanding as a dancer. The pain compelled me to learn something important on a physical level.

WHEN THE PHYSICAL ISN'T ENOUGH

This is all well and good, but injuries are not that black and white. Otherwise, with a little effort, we could fix all our injuries and be in constant perfect health. Even with a lot of effort, some injuries refuse to oblige. The healing of injuries is not always logical or consistent. Some injuries don't respond even to the most conscientious physical care. The physical, on its own, can fail to heal not because the physical is wrong but because we, as humans, are much more complex than just the physical. This is where the mental, emotional, and spiritual dimensions enter in a very valuable and healing way. More often than not, the physical is a clear demonstration of what is in the more invisible domains.

If you would like to listen to a meditation for helping to heal injuries, go to *Healing Injuries Meditation* at https://donnagoddard.com/meditations/

CHAPTER 8
Interior and Exterior Worlds

ALL ABOUT ME!

Spiritual seekers primarily focus on the interior world—thoughts, emotions, energy—rather than the exterior world. They may be highly involved in the external world, but their home is internal. Along the way, they have a progressive lessening of themselves as a separate identity, particularly as a physical entity. From a spiritual perspective, this is something we value. It means the ego is lessening its hold on us. It means we are a little less driven by ignorance than we were at the beginning of our spiritual dedication. It means we can be trusted a little more to not turn everything into, *It's all about me*. It means we can forgive more quickly because there is less of an identity to hold onto resentments. It means we are more receptive to instructions from the Source. For the seeker of Truth, the spiritual dimension is a powerful, pulsating reality.

FUNCTIONING IN THE WORLD AND IN THE STUDIO

However, we also need to function effectively within our physical bodies and the world. There may be many practical things we need to do in life. Dancing (and any other demanding form of physical activity) helps significantly with this vital aspect of balancing human and spiritual existence.

In order to strengthen the physical dimension so that it is fully functioning and workable, many spiritual seekers develop specific habits and interests that reinforce the aliveness and firing ability of their bodies. This is one of my top reasons for dancing. It helps me to stay grounded and connected with the physical world. Nothing is more physical than being in the middle of a pumping practice session with couples (primarily young) on all sides, slamming out their best, most vigorous, leg-kicking, hip-jiving routines.

A dance teacher I had earlier on often asked me how I thought something looked. I would generally reply, "I can't tell." Despite the many mirrors in a dance studio, I couldn't tell what something looked like as an objective observer. The teacher usually replied that I was not in my body enough. That's why I was in the studio! To strengthen my beingness in my body.

ENDING UP IN THE RIGHT PLACE

That teacher also said, "At some point in our dancing life, the mind stops thinking. After years of training, we no longer have to think about it. I end up in the right place. My partner ends up in the right place. It all works. I guess, for some people, that happens in meditation. For me, it happens in dancing."

As a dancer, it is important to stop thinking. If we let the mind have its way, it will never shut up. We must have enough mental awareness to know what we are doing and little enough to move with the flow. The cessation of thinking is the breeding ground for harmonious, perfect action. As onlookers, we cannot help but respond to dancers who are very present. The dancers will have drawn us into themselves and also into our own selves. The process is inclusive, not exclusive.

Dancing relieves the pain of everyday life and elevates us into a space with less thought and more nowness. Without inner silence, we can neither know ourselves, another, nor the depth of anything beautiful. One must be able to tolerate seeming nothingness to hear the silent rhythm. It warms our hearts and stretches us into beautiful forms. Its velvety smoothness effortlessly embraces us all.

Attentive presence brings us, hopefully, to the point where we are directly sitting in the stream of what is left after thought—the effortless, worryless space of harmonious presence. You could call it prayer if you had a spiritual vocabulary. But no matter, the words aren't important. What is important is an experience of that presence. It is available in any activity in life with the right mindset. Every time we are in it, a day is taken off our age. Or, if we are still young, more substance is added to our power and influence.

CHAPTER 9
Still and Sacred

STILL POINT

Advanced martial artists use *the still point* to achieve extraordinary activity, strength, and precision. Accomplished dancers also develop the ability to dance from the still point. For a long time, dance training is about correctly moving parts of the body for the relevant dance style. It starts with awareness of large, gross movement and, over the years, becomes more and more particular to the smaller, subtler movements of the body. *It's all in the details,* say the top dancers.

Eventually, the master of dance arrives at *the still point.* Movement and thought, body and mind, are so refined and intentioned that everything moves from the still point. It is not to say that the movement is calm. It may be explosive, violent, and dramatic. However, the intention is calmly focused. It is not altered by the fluctuations in the internal and external environment of the dancer. The still point is thus never lost.

The movement is part of the still.
The still is part of the movement.
The dancer can be still and still dance.
They can move and still be still.

SACRED STILLNESS

The still point in dance is the equivalent of the advanced spiritual student *ceaselessly praying*. Ceaselessly praying does not mean endlessly reciting prayers to oneself. It means that the consciousness of the spiritual student is moulded in such a way that the context of the Divine is never lost from awareness. Everything said or thought comes from that basis, even in sleep. It is living the still point as a constant, ongoing reality.

Some people find that the easiest and quickest way to reach the still point is in nature. There is a tremendous amount of stillness in the busyness of nature. If we can find the still point in nature, we can find it in our bodies. Our body is nature. The still point in nature is also the still point in us.

T. S. Eliot wrote about the still point in his poem, *Burnt Norton*. Dance is used to illustrate moments of transcendence. He infers that life, like dance, is timeless and ultimately meaningful by its pure existence.

At the still point of the turning world.
    Neither flesh nor fleshless;
Neither from nor towards; at the still point,
    there the dance is,
But neither arrest nor movement. And do
    not call it fixity,
Where past and future are gathered.
    Neither movement from nor towards,
Neither ascent nor decline. Except for the
    point, the still point,
There would be no dance, and there is only
    the dance.
I can only say, there we have been: but I
    cannot say where.
And I cannot say, how long, for that is to
    place it in time.

— T. S. ELIOT

SACRED DANCE

Sufism is the mystic pathway of Islam. Its goal is union with the Divine. Part of its tradition is sacred dance in sacred places. The whirling dervishes twirl continuously with one hand pointed upwards towards the Divine and the other hand pointed downwards towards Earth.

The dancing integrates body, mind, and spirit. It aims at elevating the dancer into a state of spiritual ecstasy. The mesmeric swirling of the Sufi dancers is a meditation. Anything that requires absolute attention becomes a meditation.

*Two hours in the dance studio,
if you pay attention,
is also a meditation.*

CHAPTER 10
Energy Centres

READING ENERGY

To an intuitive person, a person's energy is as readable as the clothes they wear. Indeed, most people know far more about other people than they realise. However, it is usually subconscious knowledge. The thought patterns of humans are very similar. Once we understand one person (ourselves), it is not difficult to understand others. The amount of energy people put into different thought patterns varies, thus the diversity of people.

CHAKRAS

The life force of every individual starts at the primal root chakra (base of the spine near the anal outlet) and the sacral chakra (behind the genitals). From there, it moves up to the solar plexus (the stomach area), the centre of individual will. It is what makes us ourselves. The life force then moves to the emotion and love of the heart centre. The heart is what makes us more than ourselves. After that, it travels to the higher spiritual domains of unconditional love, insight, intuition, healing, and divine inspiration via the throat, third eye, and crown centres.

ENERGY FLOW

One day, in my second year of ballroom dancing, I was doing the tango with a teacher. I suddenly became aware of how active the chakras are in dancing. I refrained from mentioning this discovery and reminded myself that dancers are generally not spiritual students versed in Eastern traditions. In ballroom hold, both bodies touch or almost touch at numerous energy centres, including the hands. In dancing, it is not expressed in terms of chakras but in terms of body parts. Hands and chakras are access points for energy flow between people.

The energy centres play a significant role in how people relate to each other—for better and worse. Ballroom dancing is a couple-related activity, reflecting all interactive human relationships. The energy centres of the individuals involved will determine who can dance well together and who cannot. Some combinations of energies make inspirational and captivating couples. Others are boring and lifeless. Some are fireworks in the traumatic rather than the creative sense.

BALLROOM BREATH

Before taking up ballroom hold, the partners stand several feet apart, preparing to dance. The leader indicates he wishes his partner to step towards him. The follower responds by walking up to the leader. They find their common centre and then move together. When I first learned this, I noticed that I naturally breathed in when preparing to walk in and breathed out once I was connected to teacher-partner. I felt that I was breathing myself into the other person's body, auric field, and our combined energy field. I assumed other dancers did the same, even if unconsciously. If I didn't do it, I felt disconnected from the person I was dancing with, and it was more challenging to read what they were asking me to do.

At that time, I had a private practice as a Spiritual Healer and Counsellor. I did a version of the *ballroom breath* in spiritual healing. I placed my hands on the client's energy centres. The energy centres are used because they are a direct way of communicating with the person's psyche. I breathed in the healing power of the invisible Divine and breathed out into the person's energy field. Yoga, likewise, is grounded in the breath. Every yogic movement is synchronised with a breath in or a breath out. It is never random. Breath is considered the basis of our existence.

ASSISTANCE FROM BEYOND

One afternoon while dancing, I remembered an old necklace given to me decades before. It had an image of Mary, the mother of Jesus. It was given to me by a boyfriend when we were around twenty. I decided to wear it to my lessons and classes. Each time I touched it, I asked Mary to help me to dance well. When I told my daughter about it, she joked, "Umm, I don't think Mary was a latin dancer." Probably not, but it didn't matter.

Many people have no connection to Mary, and such a request would be meaningless to them. However, we can ask for help from any spiritual figure, and we will get help.

We can also ask deceased loved ones. We can ask living teachers whom we do not physically see. We can ask God directly. We can ask any energetic life force. It is all the same powerful energy field that wishes to help us, and it is much closer than we realise. You can find your own dancing Gods, visible and invisible, to help you against the demons you meet on the dance floor. The worst demons you will ever encounter are always the ones who reside inside you.

CHAPTER 11
Ballroom and Latin

ASKING FOR WHAT WE WANT

Some years ago, I was thrilled to be accepted for lessons by a ballroom teacher who was an accomplished dancer and a lovely man. He was fully booked and only gave half-hour lessons. I was grateful to be able to have lessons with him, but half an hour once a week was just not enough for me. I was used to longer lessons, and it was my only opportunity to dance ballroom in a way that I enjoyed.

At the end of my first lesson, I decided to be brave and ask for what I wanted. I was at the bottom of the heap, a brand-new student of his and an inexperienced ballroom dancer. Nevertheless, I thought he wouldn't know what I wanted if I didn't ask. When I asked him, he laughed out loud. He was polite and didn't mean to laugh, but the idea seemed ridiculous. He looked at me oddly, shook his head, and said quietly but definitely, "Ah...no."

I took it in my stride. I knew the risk of asking. We have to be willing to accept:

- No.
- Not at this time.
- I'll think about it, but probably not.

We have to be willing to be embarrassed. We have to have enough push or life force to move forward.

Three weeks later, at the end of the lesson, my teacher said without warning, "Did you say you wanted an hour lesson?"

I looked at him in surprise and ventured a hesitant but expectant, "Yes?"

"Starting next week," he replied with a calm and unreadable face, "you can have 4 till 5."

I got what I wanted. And in the short space of three weeks. It allowed me to progress much more quickly than I otherwise would have. Besides, it was great fun.

BODY TO BODY BALLROOM

During my formative years of latin and ballroom dancing, I developed specific ways of approaching each style. In both, I tried to have lessons with the best teachers available to me, weighted with my feeling of compatibility with their nature. When I danced with my ballroom teacher, I tried to meld with their physical movement and energy. As ballroom hold means body-to-body contact, the partners must move as one unit. I would, in large part, use my teacher's confidence, experience, and power as a male dancer to compensate for my dancing shortcomings. Of course, one must outgrow this reliance on the teacher. Skilled female dancers are highly independent and centred in their own bodies. Nevertheless, it is how I tried to overcome my inexperience, improve most quickly (by getting a feel for the flow of the movement), and have the best interim experience. I think it did all of that.

DRAMA, DISTRESS, AND LATIN DANCE

Latin was a different story. It's not body-on-body contact. One has to stand on one's own two feet, or one foot as the case may be. I always had a barely concealed feeling of being, frankly, pathetic, even though, in the grand scheme of things, I don't think I was. After the distressing loss of a dancing arrangement (dancing losses are often dramatically distressing!), something changed in me in regard to latin. Over the following weeks, I would look at myself in the mirror and say, *All in all, I'm not that bad.* I stood up straighter, put my shoulders down, put my weight into my standing leg, and moved. All of these are important for being grounded in latin. From that moment on, my progress took a different curve. Latin became a love, not a losing battle. I never again felt that I couldn't do it. In fact, I decided to put all of my limited dancing money and energy into latin and dropped ballroom.

CONFIDENCE

In dancing and life, if we tell ourselves that we are incompetent, it will not work. We will not be able to put our weight squarely into anything if we are silently repeating to ourselves:

- Be careful.
- Don't commit too heavily to that.
- You already look stupid.
- Other people are so much better than you.
- Come now, you don't trust yourself to be in that position.

We have to have confidence in ourselves. However, a strong "healthy" ego will only ever get us so far. There is much in life that cannot be altered, in the slightest, by a vibrant ego. Learning the limits of the ego and when to put it in its place is pivotal to happiness and long-term success.

SURRENDER

Surrender is ultimately humility. It makes life peaceful and harmonious. Insisting, reacting, blaming, and holding onto things prevent life from evolving. They make us stuck. Surrender says:

—I don't know everything.
—It's entirely possible that I know very little.
—Perhaps I could let the Higher Power help with the direction of my life, that of my loved ones, and even that of my enemies.

Surrender says *yes* to life rather than the million *nos* that tumble out of our consciousness. A healthy amount of *No* is a way of protecting our ego and its boundaries. However, too much negative and the positive of life gets lost in the armed and dangerous force of the no-army.

Surrender also stops asking the question, *Why is this*

happening? It stops asking for explanations and accepts *what is* until *what is* changes into another *what is*. Surrender is how we move from a strong ego to that nameless quality that makes some people beautiful, resilient, unusual, and powerful in a non-egoic way.

CHAPTER 12
Fulfilling Our Potential

NOT BY ACCIDENT

Sometimes, I had a particular conversation with myself on the way to dancing.

"I must be the luckiest person alive," I said.

"Why?" I asked, thinking it was a rather grandiose statement.

"Because I get to dance."

Most people wouldn't think they were the luckiest person ever because they could go dancing. Even if they loved dancing, they would often be thinking about all the problems with dancing—their progress or stagnation, injuries, future, dance partners, teachers, students, what they could afford or not, and opportunities.

We don't have desires by accident. Good desires are planted in us because we are meant to follow them, explore them, wrestle with them, and have them form us. If we do this and do it in the right way, the result is happiness. If we do anything in the right way, the result is happiness.

HAPPINESS

The happiness doesn't come from the activity. It comes from aligning with our deeper Self. We will have ultimate faith in ourselves because the faith is in our larger Self, which has a mighty backing. Our smaller self can be so petty and vulnerable. More often than not, it is competitive, nasty, insecure, worried, and highly jealous. Our deeper Self looks on all these traits as childish. It is interested in the good of all, knowing that such is our greatest assurance and protection. It doesn't talk shallow, empty words with divisive, empty smiles. The well-being of one (even if that one is oneself) is not separated from the well-being of all.

Although it serves us not to be delusional about what we are capable of, we are often surprised by what we can do when we commit to it without fear. Other times, we must live with our limitations or destiny and find joy in what we can do with what we have been given. To believe in ourselves doesn't mean building ourselves up with unrealistic thoughts of how marvellous we will be with little evidence to support our theoretical greatness. But, nor does it mean to belittle ourselves and feel worthless. At some level, we are instinctively aware of the gifts we have been given and their extent. They will seek expression for our whole life until they have enough room to move.

BELIEVING IN OURSLEVES

Believing in ourselves is highly impactful on our development and happiness. However, the typical approach to it is flawed. Mostly, what people mean when they talk about believing in themselves is that they are better than others—

particularly those known to them. Human nature constantly compares itself to others to determine how it is doing. The problem is obvious. There will always be people better than us in any area of life. It is a never-ending path with only momentary success here and there. Further, what we give out returns to us in like. We will be living in an uncomfortable world where that which benefits one does not benefit all. There will be smiling assassins everywhere.

Fortunately, we don't need to be better than anyone else to be happy. We do, however, need to fulfil our potential. If we do not, we will feel restless and incomplete. If we work towards fulfilling our specific potential, we will feel satisfied. We will not feel starving. We will not be grabbing, moaning, or thinking about abandoning ship. We will not be unduly concerned when things don't go our way. We will have patience with ourselves, other people, and the process of life. We will feel that our progression is inevitable because we have aligned with what can only lead to success.

FULFILLING OUR POTENTIAL

To be happy, we must fulfil our innate potential. Otherwise, we will feel frustrated at some level. In fulfilling ourselves, we will naturally contribute something of worth to the world. Selfish ambition, whether blatant or secret, destroys many a friendship and many a career. Selfish ambition cannot help but see others as competition. If someone else is succeeding, we think that means we are not, or perhaps not as well as them. Dedication to the good of all, including ourselves, takes the ill will out of competitive thinking and makes the way to success smoother than we could otherwise orchestrate. We will have God/Good on our team.

To follow our destiny and have generosity and goodwill towards others gives us fearless confidence. We know that we will have our place in life and that it will bring us enjoyment and satisfaction. We will not be afraid to pursue our path with all the energy and determination we can draw into our short lifetime. When things go well, we will be gracious and grateful. When they do not, we will be hopeful. We will neither puff up with pride nor blame ourselves with recriminations of failure. Not only does such an approach save us from the never-ending stresses of competitive and ill-willed human interaction, but it makes our life a prayer.

We can accept everything good with open hands, but those hands need not grasp and cling with fear. We open our palms Heavenward with thanks that we have been given every beautiful gift that has come our way. We will not overly grieve that which changes. Sadness will not become our constant buddy but an occasional visitor we patiently entertain, knowing that the visitor will soon be gone. We will not resent the success of others. What blesses one blesses all.

In practising these attitudes, an irrepressible, alive, and glowing radiance grows within us. It protects us from innumerable human problems and is a healing balm. It brings relief to a world with much brutality on all levels. We should claim our inheritance of spiritual beauty. It is our life task to align with that beauty more fully and release all the ugliness that seems to get in the way.

CREATIVITY

Creative pursuits are most rewarding when seen as an ongoing way of being in the world. They are an avenue for fulfilling one's potential and a way of being of service by sharing what we love and feel drawn to. This removes the fuel from self-driven ambition and takes the steam out of competitive thinking. We lose the fear that we will not have a place. We lose the egotistical pride that frequently accompanies achievement. We do not cling tightly to what is good. Nor do we overly grieve what passes. We do not resent others' successes. Nor are we afraid to pursue our own.

All is graciously and gratefully given over to that which is the essence of Life and is the rightful owner of all true action and talent. The success and beauty of the endeavour are heightened. Anxiety, fear, and the precarious confidence that accompanies egoic pursuits are disempowered. Ego-driven ambition is replaced with gratitude for what we love. The creative impetus is given every opportunity to express itself unfettered by human complications. There grows a quiet, alive, confident, glowing radiance. It moves and moulds us, uniting us with our awakening nature, feeding the little shoot until its full majestic nature takes hold.

WE ARE ONE

We all have our destinies to fulfil. Each one must play their part. We will then be happy, and that is all we need. We can turn everything we do into a prayer. Instead of feeling inadequate or unlucky, we can feel a part of the grand flow of Creation, which encompasses everyone. We belong to it and benefit richly from that belonging. The flowering of our potential will be significantly enhanced.

All life forms value their own existence and the reaching of their potential. Awareness of this helps us move from the natural egocentricity that accompanies being human.

Instead of constantly seeing our own life and needs as being of primary importance, we soften that view with an appreciation of the life value and needs of everyone and everything. Respect and goodwill replace comparison and ill will.

Our gifts and talents are not only given to us for our enjoyment and fulfilment but also for the benefit of other people. Our talent does not have to be Olympic or world-class standard. It just has to be a genuine appreciation for some aspect of life that we particularly feel drawn to. Even participating in a hobby or talent that no one sees uplifts the world significantly by the sincerity, gratitude, and purity of intention we put into it. All of life is energetic. All thoughts and actions are energetically experienced by the world, at some level, whether we intend it or not. Every loving thought contributes to the world. Every act of beauty and harmonious participation helps the world to raise its vibration.

By reducing the self-confirmatory aspects of any activity, we also reduce the anxiety attached to it. If we do well, we thank God that we can participate in something wonderful, the essence of which is always Divine. The happiness of knowing that is our reward. If something goes badly, we do not take it personally, but we realise that our expression is not yet complete in that area, and we try again. All mistakes are lessons, and all achievements demonstrate God's presence. We are here for God. And as God is love, we are here for Love's expression. We are One. The beauty in one person is shared by all. The life path of one individual blesses everyone. The expression of Life neither originates within a single human nor belongs to that person exclusively.

Life is energy,
and as such,
it belongs to all,
reaches all,
and blesses all.

CHAPTER 13
Pas De Deux

*Dancing, at its best,
is independence and intimacy
in balance.*

FEAR, FUN, FURY

Dancers dance because they learn things about themselves through dancing. They develop parts of themselves that are not yet finished. It's not necessarily about enjoyment, although enjoyment is always pleasant and fun when it happens. It may be confronting, infuriating, depressing, or even debilitating. We are generally not learning the thing we think we are, and even less the thing we want. Dancing helps us to become balanced as a whole entity. It helps us to grow, and we should let it do so. We should be grateful for what makes us grow, even though it may be a love-hate relationship with the things responsible for that growth. Dancing is letting a little piece of life come through us, together with another person who is gracious enough to want to share a little piece of life with us.

When I was a child, I sometimes dreamed about being a ballerina. I wasn't part of the corps de ballet. Nor was I a star soloist. It was always pas de deux. The critical thing seemed to be relating to another human being as a dancer and for something beautiful and meaningful to come out of it. As a child, I could not express it in those words. Nevertheless, my subconscious mind must have known what it wanted because the dream never changed.

As dancers, we dance with many different people—our own age, older, younger, the opposite sex, the same sex, straight, gay. However, these are only the surface differences. The fundamental dynamic of the dance situation is that two separate energy systems are trying to create something together. Neither can do it without the other. It can bring pleasure, pain, fear, fun, and fury. To dance with another person is a privilege. To create anything with someone else is a privilege. In its most sincere form, it cannot be bought. It is freely given as the gift of oneself. It should be respected.

DRIVING OUR DANCING

How we relate to those we dance with is as varied as how we relate to people in ordinary life. We all have default personalities, but we must alter them depending on who we are trying to connect with. We have to adjust so that we can communicate effectively. What we communicate nonverbally is more vital than what we say out loud. It will significantly influence the outcome.

When I taught my teenagers to drive, I told them, "People drive like who they are. Angry people drive angrily.

Crazy people drive like lunatics. Calm people drive safely. Attentive people are aware drivers. Dreamy people don't pay attention."

My son tells me that when I get into a deep conversation, I drive slower and slower as the conversation gets more absorbing until I am well below the speed limit and probably most annoying to other drivers.

Like driving, people dance like who they are. If we are drawn to dance with someone and have the opportunity to do so, we must try to accommodate and appreciate the other person, as they must try to accommodate and appreciate us. If they cannot see us and who we are, or if we cannot see them, then that is not a good start. First, we must SEE each other. That is less common than one might imagine.

My dance teacher decided to try and reduce the arguing that frequently accompanied the practice sessions. He asked his training couples to stand in a circle and say something they sincerely appreciated about their partner. They did what he asked, and a sense of peace settled in the room. He reminded them that they did not know how long they would have their dance partner or even their dancing career, and it would be good to be grateful. Appreciation goes a long way in healing and transforming stressed relationships. The rest of the practice was indeed calm, cooperative, and harmonious.

NEED AND NEEDINESS

There is a difference between seeking and asking for what we genuinely need from other people and neediness as a character trait. A lady at a dance studio I attended had her lesson around the same time as me. She was well-dressed, refined, eager to learn, and grateful to her teacher. She never looked directly at me. She didn't respond if I smiled at her. I felt she must be absorbed in her lesson and didn't want to engage with anyone else. One day, I decided to speak to her. I realised that she was completely blind. I was impressed by her ability to cope. She asked for help when needed but tried to be as independent and gracious as possible.

Overcoming the challenge of polio, earlier in his promising political career, Franklin Roosevelt became four-time president of the most powerful nation in the world. He couldn't walk a step without pain and effort, but he had no neediness. He focused on what he had to give. Even though Roosevelt was in a wheelchair, he had an attractive presence. Interestingly, one can be an attractive person by one's inner qualities alone.

We tend to be repelled by needy people. They make us cringe. We find neediness offensive because our vulnerability to it repulses us. There is a hidden part of us (for some, not so secret) that would love to crawl up in a little ball on the sofa with blankie and call Mummy to feed us and Daddy to protect us. Most of us refrain from doing that, at least most of the time.

Emotional and spiritual maturity is the most trustworthy assurance against neediness. It gives us calm confidence. Attractive people are not needy. There are life principles we can lean on so as not to lean too heavily on others. We gladly accept everything positive that comes to us from other people. However, we do not demand, coerce, beg, or passively manipulate people into giving us anything. We get what we need by allowing the positive principles of Life to guide our steps.

RISK

It is because people are different that something alive and interesting can happen in dance and life. It is fragile. In dancing, not only is technique and capability to be considered but there is also the highly impactful field of individual natures.

- **Depth** or lack of it.
- Amount of **fire** inside.
- Presence or absence of **calmness.**
- The quality of **mental lucidity.**
- **Emotional openness** and transparency
- Willingness to bring one's **soul** to the table to see what the other will do with it.

All high risk. Everything beautiful and powerful is (or at least was at various points) high risk. Along the way, we gain patience and perseverance by accepting the ebb and flow, ups and downs of human life. We can gain an underlying spiritual equilibrium by riding the waves with as little resistance as possible.

PARTNERING

We bring all that we are to any partnership and certainly to dancing. The energy field around each person touches the other's auric field even without touching bodies. The eyes are the transparent waterway to the soul. Do not the eyes tell a million stories? Conscious of it or not, we want to extend ourselves through this contact with another soul.

If we bring neediness to an independent
    person,
they will think we are pathetic.
If we do not need enough,
they will feel they have nothing to give us.
If we push too hard into someone's fears,
they will run away.
If we don't push enough, nothing will
    grow.

If we do not give a woman freedom to be
    herself,
if we dominate her so that she cannot move,
if we give her nothing to lean on,
if we do not let her know she can trust us to
    do our part,
then she will not flourish.

If we do not give a man our trust,
if we do not let him know that we
    need him,
if we do not let him fulfil his responsi-
    bilities,
if we do not let him have space to grow,
then he will not feel like a man.

Both must ask, and if that doesn't work,
demand strength from the other.
This is the beauty and power of it—
the wonderful, exhilarating, funny,
humbling, painful, surprising, enlightening
beauty and power of our lives together.

CHAPTER 14
Demand and Supply

SIMPLE ECONOMICS

In many dance forms, including ballroom dancing, men rule. They rule not because of some innate quality that makes them better rulers but because of the principles of demand and supply. There are more female dancers than males, so a good male dancer is valuable. Simple economics. Nothing wrong with that. However, as one would expect, good male dancers can become selfish and controlling. Also, as expected, women can become submissive add-ons. I'm not saying that it's men's fault. Many women would do the same if the dancing shoe were on the other foot. Besides, I love men—more than women. Probably because they love me—more than women. Jokes aside, it's not anyone's fault because it's what human nature does to protect its interests (given half a chance).

SEDUCTION

Along with the power, some male dancers become highly seductive creatures. Not seductive to get someone to bed (although that would sometimes be the case) but seductive to get a base of fans who can then be used for various purposes. The bait of the seduction is something more valuable than sex. It is *the possibility of being danced with* which most female dancers would, hands down, take over sex. Due to sheer numbers, the lure is generally an unconsummated promise, but it still works well. Or does it?

The whole thing can be amusing, frustrating, or heartbreaking. It is always short-sighted. There is a better way for men and women to relate and get what they genuinely want in dance and life. Honesty, authenticity, humility, respect, and courage are uncommon qualities, but they are worth developing because they work. They work without manipulation. They work without anyone losing their self-esteem. They work without hurting another person.

NOT MORE OR LESS

The best goal is for no one to end up less, no one to end up more, no one to lose, and no one to win while the other suffers. The partnership and both people will be transformed along the way. That's an interesting and worthy partnership. The struggle will be real. The ego can get extremely nasty, destructive, and savage when its whole foundation is being shaken, but all the carry-on is not much more than a childish tantrum that will be happily outgrown when one realises it is pointless. Whatever genuinely brings people together positively and with heart is a powerful force for good. Nothing of actual worth is ever gained by force, and nothing of substance is ever lost by listening to our higher self.

FOR A MOMENT

For female dancers, it helps to see ourselves as whole dancers already. We don't need another person to enjoy dancing, even in couple-based ballroom dancing. The main thing is to dance, move, learn, grow, and be open to anything that takes our interest and helps us develop. For those times when someone does want to dance with us, and when we would like to dance with them, we can accept it graciously for what it is. It is an expression of life that is shared just for a moment. If there is another moment, well and good. If there isn't, there will undoubtedly be different moments of another type. The moments will come. Come and go, come and go. We only have moments, but moments bring us to timelessness.

CHAPTER 15
The Stalls of Life

VISITING THE PAST

At certain moments in life, our psyche will try to clean up piles of unprocessed matter in our consciousness. Our soul always wants to help us move ahead. It takes every opportunity to release anything that needs healing.

After never showing the slightest interest in ice skating, my teenage son took a sudden interest in it. His paternal grandparents were champions and show skaters, and his father could skate as soon as he could walk. My son spent much of his early life in an ice rink because his father was a coach, I was a skater (at that time), and my older children were also skaters. This child knew the nature of an ice rink from in utero. However, his skating life happened to him before memory took hold, so he could remember almost nothing of it. I had not been in an ice rink myself for nine years as I had transferred from skating to ballroom dancing.

Our first visit back to this world naturally brought up many memories. As soon as I walked into the rink, I smelt the familiar damp air, heard the sound of blade against ice, and felt the biting cold on my face. Without setting foot on the ice, I could feel the body memory of skating rising in my body. I could feel the sensation of stroking and pushing into the ice, the open-hip, backward gliding motion, the stretching sensation.

All these types of returns are valuable healing opportunities. They become checkpoints for our soul to look at itself. Life will tend to arrange things for us of its own accord. After all, life is on our side and much cleverer than us. We may reconnect with those we have loved, fix a few things up, communicate some previously unspoken words, check the state of those we have left behind, and look at our progress since we belonged in that other different world. Our very being there will tend to sort out some karma.

RETURN PHENOMENON

If our current life is not going well or we are under the stress of major responsibilities, our psyche will generally not want to add to the stress by putting us in a challenging situation that further depletes our energy. An exception would be if we are going through a significant breaking-up of our thought patterns. A return to the past may be part of what is already a substantial and vital shake-up. Usually, however, our psyche does not try to heal or deal with extra things when we are busy surviving. The *return* phenomenon is for healing, so we should follow its instinctive course. As suddenly as it appeared, the whole thing can have run its course in one way or another, and we will be free to move forward in life, having lightened our spirit.

SORTING PILES

Returning to the past is a breathing space. It is like opening the doors to a forgotten cupboard, pulling everything out, wiping it, sorting what is inside, and only putting back what we genuinely want to keep. Our family rule for clean-outs was three bags:

1. one for rubbish
2. one for charity
3. one to keep

We can do the same for these types of visits:

1. throw out the debris from our minds that we no longer wish to keep
2. give others our generous thoughts of gratitude and love
3. keep the memories we want to treasure in a safe place.

TANTRUMS

Nothing gets healed without a willingness to forgive. Who does not carry a million scars from being human? It's inevitable. Without forgiveness, memories that come up have no viable place to go but back inside us. Without forgiveness, any visit to the past will tend to be painful.

Many of the hurts we experience in life come from our inner child. It is the inner child who is so fragile and easily hurt. It has little resilience and will tend to react when things don't go its way. It can have a hissy-fit, stamp its proverbial feet, threaten to run away, lie, and all manner of not-very-mature responses. The more the hidden, vulnerable, and fragile child is awakened in a situation, the more it will tend to react badly.

The inner child houses our craziness, but it also houses the place where we love most openly and trustingly. It is, in fact, the very place we start to love and heal. Understanding this helps us to forgive.

> An open heart does not hold onto pain—
> it drifts on through.
> An open heart heals quickly—
> it breathes fresh air.
> An open heart does not lose its bright
>   spirit—
> it scars little and gives a lot.

SITTING IN THE STALLS

A few months into our skating return, I looked across the ice rink from where I was sitting, and what I saw brought tears to my eyes. It was a simple thing—just a boy and a girl becoming a young man and a young woman.

My son was still very much a beginner skater. Skating is a technically demanding sport. It takes years to become competent. However, even though he was a beginner, he was a *male* figure skater. Anyone in the skating or dancing world knows what that means. A good male skater or dancer is highly valued and is in great demand. And so it was not surprising that from the moment we arrived, all the young female skaters were aware of my son's presence. It's great for the male ego!

An adorable and very accomplished girl skater instantly sized up the situation and quickly made friends with us.

One day, early on, she was practising near my still-flailing son. She took hold of my son's hand and helped him with his skating—giving him tips and hoping like hell that he would hurry up and improve.

When I first glimpsed this picture, there was something very moving about it—the fragile, hopeful reaching out. So many things could interfere to cause the whole thing to come crashing down. Yet, the two young people were present to each other. As an ex-skater and current dancer, I understood the girl's heartfelt desire to move/skate/dance with another human being.

I wondered if anyone else noticed. Could anyone else feel the beauty in the situation? It seemed to me such a palpable thing, as if it was singing a happy song to everyone in the rink. At least one other person did notice. When my son's coach passed me, he nodded in their direction and said, "I think there is a little friendship growing there." I saw the same touched look on his face that I could not help feeling in my heart. When young people first taste the sort of love that forges friendships and forms love affairs, we are reminded that the world is as it should be. That thing that keeps saving humanity—the human desire for connection, friendship, and love—is alive and well.

A million things can go wrong in our friendships and relationships. A million things can go wrong if you are a dancer trying to dance with another person. But if we don't try, if we don't throw ourselves into life with abandon, if we don't somehow believe that whatever happens, we will be better off, then we may as well get off life's dance floor and sit in the stalls watching other people. It will be safer, but if it's like the ice rink, you will end up very cold.

PART TWO

Stories in Stories

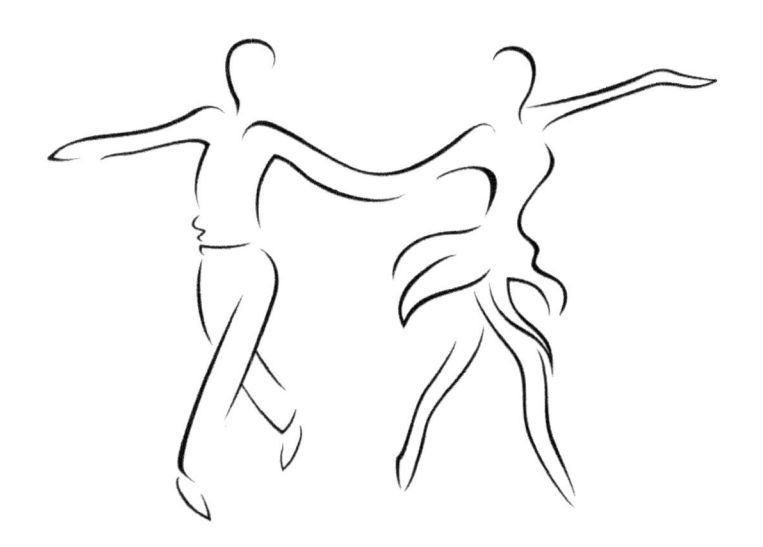

CHAPTER 16
Dance Thread

I have two adult fiction series:

1. *Waldmeer Series: A Spiritual Fiction Series*
2. *Nanima Series: Spiritual Fiction*

Although neither is specifically about dance, they both have numerous dance parts. They are the dance stories within the main stories. Whether in nonfiction or fiction, dance is a wonderful medium to immerse oneself. It is a great place to put characters because they can have their pleasures, joys, problems, and lessons within the dynamic context of the dance world. I have used various dance forms —ballroom, ballet, ice skating, and others. Here is the dance thread running through the two series.

CHAPTER 17
Waldmeer Series
A SPIRITUAL FICTION SERIES

WALDMEER (BOOK 1)

HAPPY MOMENTS

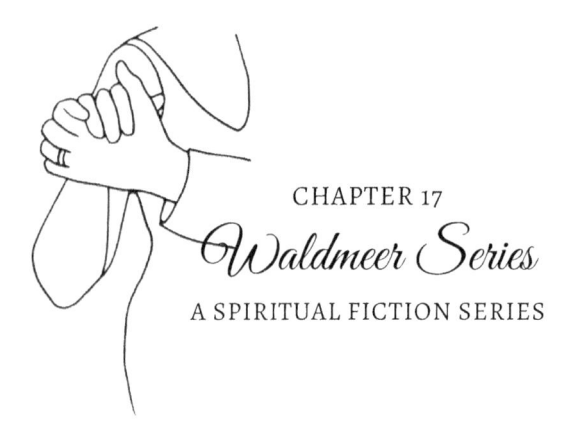

Dance first appears in the *Waldmeer Series* at the end of *Waldmeer (Book 1)*. It insisted on getting its foot in before the book closed its curtain. The protagonist, Amira, and her love interest, Gabriel, started attending a local city dance class. This first glimpse into dance focuses on its power to create happy moments—timeless moments when all is forgotten except the dance. The endless complaints and struggles are erased by being present in the calmness and unity. It is a spiritual experience because it is unifying, healing, happifying, and uplifting.

The dancing would always save the situation. It wasn't all of the dancing. Much of it was spent with Gabriel telling Amira what she was doing wrong. It was the moments, the precious moments. The moments when no one was complaining, blaming, thinking about past hurts, or fearing future ones. It was those moments of simply being present to another person, moments of being grateful. Gratitude for another being, appreciation for life. Those moments made their relationship.

CIRCLES OF SEPARATION (BOOK 3)

MINDLESSNESS

Dancing reappears more substantially in *Circles of Separation (Book 3)*. Amira and Gabriel moved to the country, Amira to Waldmeer and Gabriel to Darnall. Gabriel told Amira that Darnall College (where he worked as an art teacher) was running a ballroom dancing program with the Dementia Unit of the local hospital. They needed a fill-in teacher for one night. Amira hesitated but said, "Okay. Why not? It'll be fun, and they won't be able to remember if we are right or wrong." And so began a period of teaching ballroom dancing to the Dementia Unit. The marvellous thing about dementia was that it got rid of the logical mind and allowed the other-dimensionality of dance to spread its wings.

One of the class participants was Wolfgang, an elegant gentleman in his mid-eighties whose wife, Madeline, was in the Dementia Unit. Earlier in their lives, they danced ballroom competitively and often went to Blackpool. Gabriel asked them to dance for the class. Wolfgang took hold of his wife's hand, and as they danced, he seemed to be regaining part of Madeline. This demonstrates how dance can transcend logical, time-bound, and place-specific limitations.

ELECTRIC ENERGY

Wolfgang referred to the energy that passes between people when they dance as electricity.

> "I remember," said Wolfgang, "the first time I danced with Madeline. We were having a tryout. Neither of us was very good at that stage. We did the cha-cha, and it went okay. Then came rumba, the dance of love. A few steps into the dance, Madeline held her hand on my stomach. I was slightly surprised because she was a shy and proper young lady. It seemed a little forward. Not that I minded. Oh, no. You see, it was the way she touched me. I felt electricity in my body. I didn't know if other people felt it when they danced with her or only me. Either way, I wanted her."

WHAT DANCING REALLY IS

He viewed the essence of competitive dance as something beyond winning or losing.

"We were quite a duo back then," said Wolfgang. "I remember at Blackpool that my white jacket caused a big stir amongst all the conventional black ones. It upset the apple cart, alright. Some of the judges loved it, and some hated it. We didn't care. Who cares about judges when you have each other and you are creating something together? Winning only matters when you don't have what dancing really is."

NOT DEAD YET

Two months passed. The class came to an equilibrium of its own accord. Lacking technical knowledge, Gabriel and Amira tried to transfer the feeling of each dance and give their students an immersive experience. That meant turning the music up and dancing enthusiastically with the class members in, more or less, the appropriate style. Gabriel would yell out encouragement and random advice above the music.

"Keep going. You're doing great," yelled Gabriel. "Jive is meant to be fun. Have fun, folks. Let's go. Go, go, go."

Everyone loved it, and they did have fun.

"You're not dead yet," he called out. "Keep those legs moving."

That was always greeted with peals of laughter. It was a fresh joke to most each time they heard it. Even the staff didn't seem to tire of the joke. Some of the staff who joined the frivolities felt more alive than they did for the rest of their week. Amira was the only one who would look sideways at Gabriel when he repeated the joke, yet again, to which he would say, "I'm on a winner."

DATING APPS

The joint time of teaching the class gave an opportunity for Amira and Gabriel to work out some of their ongoing relationship issues. It provided a context for their coming together, moving apart, and coming together again. Like many other activities, dance allows people to connect, learn about each other, and learn about themselves without the rather orchestrated context of modern dating apps. It's the old-fashioned dating app. It is a natural, healthy, balanced context for people (young and old) to throw themselves into all sorts of relationships.

After a breakup, Amira and Gabriel began taking the class separately. It inevitably brought about the weekly response from the Dementia Unit patients that "Someone is missing," although they couldn't remember who.

PROTECT THE GIFT

Amira decided to take the class to the city to see the ballet. The ballet company had a popular pas de deux couple, Clayton and Kristel. Clayton was a vibrant, outgoing dancer whose giant leaps and entertaining stage presence won the hearts of his followers some years back. Kristel was a newer star. Her usual demeanour was far from that of a star. She was reserved and preferred her own company. She was the opposite of self-promoting. It was a wonder that she was given the prestigious lead role except that she could be captivating when she danced. She had a purity about her, and it translated into a fragile, enchanting beauty in dancing. The Directors of the ballet company were not unanimous in supporting Kristel. Many preferred the more dominant, exciting dancing of some of the fiercer female students. If it were not for the insistence of the most senior director, Kristel would not have been given the lead role.

"Kristel has dancing in her," said the director quite adamantly.

His fellow directors wondered what he thought the other students had in them.

"Our job is to protect it," he continued. "If we try to mould it, we may destroy it. Just protect it and make it feel safe. It will come out. You will see."

"And then," he added with a smile, "everyone will thank us for giving them a gift."

MAGIC OF THE MOMENT

The partnership of Clayton and Kristel had its ups and downs. If Clayton pushed too hard or ignored Kristel's gentle presence, the duet became unbalanced. Kristel would underperform and look less than the corps de ballet, and Clayton would look like a self-absorbed show-off. If they got it right, Kristel forgot herself and became entrancing, and Clayton became the strong, brilliant dancer he was. Isn't it the task of art to bring out our best self? On this occasion, they got it right. They were so together and absorbed in the dance that they became much more than their small, individual selves. The audience felt equally included in the magic of the moment. Everyone was spellbound.

On the long drive back to Darnall in the country bus, everyone was content and talked about the ballet and the gorgeous dancers until they forgot where they had been. The memory of the event may have drifted into the ether, but the feeling of beauty and hope remained inside them.

PITTOWN (BOOK 5)

FEROCIOUS DESIRE

The fifth book of the series jumps ahead twenty years and gives us a new protagonist, Merlyn, and a new love interest, Ben, a professional ballet dancer. No longer a performing dancer, he taught and choreographed at the State Ballet. Merlyn and Ben were married for three years and then separated.

Merlyn, who was not a dancer, sometimes visited her friend's cafe next door to the State Ballet. As her eyes were drawn to the magnificent sandstone building that became the home of the State Ballet eighty years ago, she thought not only about Ben but all the dancers who had walked in and out of those doors. So many dreams and aspirations, so much failure and disappointment.

> In amongst the momentary glory and inevitable change would always be the unrelenting, ferocious desire to express the soul through the mechanics of a limited body in the hope that it could bring some peace to a painful inner and outer world.

> *Maybe it's limited,* thought Merlyn. *Maybe it's a lot of work for fleeting imperfection, but along with all the dirty work, there is also love. Along with all the dirty dancing, there is also purity. Along with all the hatred, hurt, and anger, there is also healing. That is the life of a ballet company. Indeed, that is life.*

DON'T SIT IN YOUR ARSE

Being inspired, Merlyn asked Ben to teach her how to dance. As a birthday present, he gave her one lesson. It was no walk in the park.

"Stand up. Get your head up. Centre in. Eyes forward. Don't lean on me," commanded Ben. "Don't sit in your arse. Stand on your legs. Use your feet. Point them. You're rounding your shoulders. Centre in. Centre in!"

At one point, he stopped in exasperation and said, "You are dancing like a needy little child. Stand up and get out of my space!"

Merlyn would have objected, but she knew it was all perfectly true. After two hours of repetition, she managed to do a very basic pas de deux with Ben.

"Okay, that's it," said Ben. "Times up. That's more private lesson time than most dancers get."

After the million commands he had thrown at her, he was fairly sure that her dancing aspirations would have been redirected.

"How did you like it?" he asked finally.

"I loved it," said Merlyn with unashamed exhilaration.

"Oh," said Ben.

"Can we do it again?" asked Merlyn.

"No," said Ben. "Definitely not. I don't teach private lessons except to the soloists and pas de deux couples. I certainly don't teach beginners. Go to an adult ballet class."

STANDING ON OUR OWN TWO FEET

As Ben wouldn't teach her more than one lesson, Merlyn decided to be a grown-up about it and, unknown to him, took his advice. If she wanted to dance, expecting Ben to facilitate her wishes was unrealistic, unfair, and burdensome. So, she embarked on a training and education regime, which she consistently stuck to for the following year. She went to adult ballet classes, advancing from beginner to intermediate. She had private lessons with appropriate teachers who took beginners. She added to her four-day-a-week dancing program: daily walks, a weekly yoga class, and plenty of home stretching based on what she learned in yoga. As a result, her fitness, strength, and flexibility improved out of this world. Mind you, her body hurt every single day. Usually, it was simple muscle soreness. Sometimes, it was injury. However, each injury taught her something important about what not to do in dancing.

By the end of the year, she decided to surprise Ben in her birthday ballet lesson with him. As she opened the large glass doors of the sandstone ballet building, she realised that she was beginning to vaguely feel like a dancer. On the occasions Ben had seen her in the interim year, he had noticed that she was thinner and had more muscle tone, but it didn't cross his mind that she would have embarked on a dance training program without him. Not that he minded. He was rather impressed with the effort and self-reliance that it took.

DANCE: A SPIRITUAL AFFAIR

For Merlyn's part, what she enjoyed most about this year's lesson was a fleeting moment of relaxation in Ben's eyes. Instead of having to carry her for the entire dance, he could, here and there, leave her to do her part and concentrate on his own. It was fleeting, but it was there— a whisp of something new and alive. He could not have known how much that meant to her.

What is dancing other than the desire for a moment of freely-given joint creation? It takes time, but even more than time, it takes trust. Trust, not so much in another—humans are so damn changeable—but trust in the part of another that does not change. The part that is whole and happy.

❧

PRANA (BOOK 6)

SHAMBHAVI AND THE MANIPURA DANCERS

Prana (Book 6) introduces us to a new character, Shambhavi. Like Ben, he was a professional dancer, although he came from a different style. He lived in Prana Community, near Waldmeer, a dedicated spiritual community of the yogic tradition. He and his wife devoted themselves to the practices of the community, particularly the asana practices in their authentic form.

Perched on a cliff, Ajna Temple was the masterpiece of

Prana Community. Silence was maintained inside the temple. It was named after the Ajna chakra between the eyebrows (the third eye), the centre of intuition, self-assurance, and inner knowing. Although the temple was dedicated to one of the higher, more ethereal chakras, one particular group who frequented the temple was wholeheartedly dedicated to the lower chakras. They were the Manipura Dancers, founded by Shambhavi. They were wild. It was the only time that noise was allowed in the temple. They were a damn noisy lot. Noisy and wild. Everyone loved them!

BODY AND SPIRIT BALANCE

This section of the story highlights the difference between the ethereal higher chakras and the earthy lower ones. It shows how both are important to be a balanced person, a balanced spiritual seeker, and a balanced dancer.

> It was the much anticipated monthly gathering of the Manipura Dancers. The professional musicians inside Ajna Temple were beating out a strong, rhythmic pulse. Merlyn was a little surprised not only by how loud it was but also by how earthy, physical, and even sexual it was in a temple of such high spiritual vibration. Nothing was explained. The music simply throbbed, hypnotised, and seduced. What it was seducing and for what purpose, Merlyn wasn't sure.
>
> The Manipura Dancers were like Sufi dancers—wild and ecstatic. However, unlike Sufi dancers, they didn't just twirl in endless circles. They moved everywhere and with everything, especially with their hips, core, and the lower part of their bodies.

Ah, thought Merlyn, *that's why they are called the Manipura Dancers. It's the powerhouse fire element coming from the centre.*

The music, the temple, the linga, and all the bodies seemed to be committed to a process that was intrinsically familiar and also utterly mysterious.

DANCING IS MY RELIGION

One day, Shambhavi explained to Merlyn how the Manipura Dancers came to be.

"Even though I come from a dancing family, I struggled in the beginning with the yogic practices in Prana Community," said Shambhavi. "Then, one day, here in the temple, I had an idea. I turned all my dancing knowledge into yoga. That was the day the Manipura Dancers were born, and that was also how I got my name which means *something born from happiness.* They said that when I dance, something blissful comes alive in me."

GENEROSITY

Shambhavi started teaching a dance class in Waldmeer as a community outreach. He knew the initial classes would be make or break for such a small, insular town as Waldmeer. So, he brought out all his charm to try and gently win them over. Although he was way overqualified for such a class, he wanted to use the opportunity to build a bridge between Waldmeer and Prana Community. The former had always been deeply suspicious of the latter. Besides, Shambhavi not only loved to dance, but he loved to teach.

Teaching is sharing.
To be a good teacher, you have to be generous.

PURNIMA (BOOK 7)

BALANCING THE FIRE

In *Purnima (Book 7),* we meet a new character at the State Ballet, fiery Mr Peen. The State Ballet didn't normally bother with training nonprofessional adult dancers. However, Merlyn's class was a special promotional offer. The students were given a mixture of instructors—marvellous, young, current dancers or older professionals with a great deal of experience.

> Today's class was with a senior teacher, Mr Peen. He was a commanding person with an excellent dancing background. At fifty, he was still a captivating and energetic dancer. Mr Peen had a few children (spread out in age) to a few women (spread out in time). He had lived and loved. He had won and lost. He knew what he was doing. And he didn't. No one could accuse him of not trying. He was still trying. A decent, driven, principled man with a lot of fire for life. Sometimes, a little too much fire.

At Prana Community, Merlyn learned that the human body has five base elements in differing proportions: 72% water, 12% earth, 6% air, 6% ether, and 4% fire. Whenever she looked at Mr Peen, she felt that instead of 4% fire, he got 5 or 6% fire. That might not seem much of a difference, but fire is the most potent element. Even a tiny amount brings lots of power and focus to the individual's system. Too much fire and the person will start burning up, either in the physical body or in their more subtle bodies. She reached out to touch Mr Peen's hand so that some of the water element (which was strong in her) would flow into him as a balance.

DEVOTION INSPIRES DEVOTION

Shambhavi convinces his Waldmeer students to participate in the next Manipura Dancers full moon performance in Ajna Temple. He said he wanted them to experience firsthand the joy of sharing dance with others.

> "I don't care about your technical level or fitness," said Shambhavi. "Of course, I would like it to be as good as possible, and we are going to keep working on that, but mostly, I want you to know what it is like to take the dance inside you and present it in a way that other people can see and appreciate."

With his perfect body, perfect training, and perfect career, Shambhavi could have been forgiven for being disinterested in the motley lot of country dancers of all ages and abilities that faced him every week in Waldmeer. Yet, there was none of that in him. That is why the women (without exception) said yes to his project, although it would have frightened the life out of most of them.

The one thing that inspires fearless devotion
  in followers is devotion from their leader.

NOT MUCKING AROUND

Before the performance in Ajna Temple, Shambhavi spoke to the audience about why their dancing took such an earthy, sensual form.

> "It may seem odd to some of you," said Shambhavi, "that the Manipura Dancers deliberately (and almost exclusively) focus on the lower chakras of the body. All the odder perhaps because we are dancing in the pure and unique setting of Ajna Temple. The three energy centres we concentrate on are *Muladhara* (at the base of the spine), *Svadhisthana* (behind the genitals), and *Manipura* (at the naval). Together, these centres control the health and balance of our basic physical needs—food, sleep, and sex. They control our ability to be creative. They give us emotional stability and enough personal power to achieve what we want. They may be chakras that align with the lower elements of life, but without them, all our work in the more spiritual and intuitive centres would be fraught with difficulties.

So, please, do not think that we dancers are just mucking around, having fun, doing not much of any use. We are building the foundational structure so that all the higher energies will find a suitable home in us."

CHAPTER 18
Nanima Series
SPIRITUAL FICTION

NANIMA (BOOK 1)

MASTERS

Dance first appears in the *Nanima Series* when the main character, Maliyan, a fifty-year-old woman who returned to her hometown in the country, discovers that a ballroom dancing studio is opening in Nanima.

> "Ballroom dancing is one of those wonderful dance forms that has an active place for all age groups," said the woman. "I have friends who do competitive ballroom dancing as Masters, and they are in their seventies."
>
> "Does being in Masters make you a master," asked Maliyan, "or does it just mean you are old?"

INSTANT LOVE AFFAIR

Ballroom dancing was not a new venture for Maliyan. She had been involved with it for ten years between the ages of thirty and forty.

> When she first started dancing, it was an instant love affair—with dance. Dance ignited something in her that was different to everything else inside her. A long-lost part of herself was breathing again. She wasn't sure how long it had been lost but was glad to have it re-found. The fact that it was also good for her health was an auxiliary to her pure pleasure in moving her body. Add another person, and it multiplies the joy, at least at various points along the way.

LOVE LESSONS

As ballroom dancing is couple dancing, it brings up many of the same pleasures and problems as life relationships. The dance relationship's close (but usually nonsexual) nature is conducive to advancing people's understanding of themselves and life if they take the opportunity to learn from it.

> Maliyan was given several opportunities to partner with people. Her favourite partner was during the last few years of her dancing. As often happens with favourites, it had a less-than-favourite ending. He was a good male dancer, better than her, which is worth a lot. After a while, he fell in love with her. After more of a while, she fell in love with him.

They fell in love in somewhat different ways. He fell in love in the usual way. She fell in love in a conscious way. One of the reasons she did so was because he was married. That is always problematic. However, it's not overly problematic if you fall in love consciously because what you want is different.

BODY TALK

Unresolved mental problems get stuck in our bodies and try to talk to us through pain if the subtler ways have failed to reach us. Although Maliyan was excited to dance again, she developed a back issue that prevented her from starting.

You would think the connection between a new and old dance situation would be obvious to Maliyan, but we are masters at not seeing the obvious. So, our body takes on the connection for us. Once we relieve it of this responsibility, it usually jumps for joy and jumps right out of whatever physical predicament it had to acquire on our behalf. The karmic dumping ground of our body is the storehouse of many memories. Bodies have their own highly effective way of doing the talking.

DANCING HUNTER

After dealing with the inner issue enough for the physical one to settle, Maliyan was able to begin classes at the Nanima dance school. She met a dancer whom she called the *Dancing Hunter* because of the incongruity of his dancing sensitivity and his love of hunting.

Not only did the Dancing Hunter lead Maliyan beautifully, but he also led everyone beautifully. His experience and sensitivity allowed him to adjust his lead from the very beginners to the more experienced dancers. He made the clumsy women more graceful, the flighty ones more grounded, the aggressive ones more feminine, and the insecure ones more confident. He gave the best dancers the opportunity to spread their dancing wings.

There was something else Maliyan noticed about his partnering skills. She didn't mind him touching her.

More, she caught herself reaching out to touch him. She wondered if the other women had the same response. After looking closely, she could see that they did. Women only do that when they feel no need to protect themselves. It is a sense of trust that if they let their guard down, they will not be led astray.

TOUCH

Touch is a conveyor belt of energy. It has a binding nature and can be as deep and impactful in simple, noninvasive physical interactions as it is in sexual interactions.

Maliyan remembered her last dance partner. They didn't have a sexual relationship. However, the mere act of holding hands (and dancing is all about hand-holding) at frequent, regular intervals over several years was as binding as sex. The act of continued physical proximity combined with emotional connection is highly binding. If both links are present, the bond between two people will be cemented in their consciousness and the very structure of their bodies. They are holding each other's spirit as well as each other's body. If the relationship ends, the partners will suffer and grieve as much as they would the loss of a lover. That is how powerful touch is when it is combined with emotion. No trifling plaything!

GEBOOR (BOOK 2)

MEDITATION

The Nanima dance school unexpectedly closed, and Maliyan arranged to use the empty studio to practice in until it had a new renter. There was no electricity, so she used it when it wasn't too hot or dark. Unlike lessons and classes, a well-organised, attentive practice can become meditative in its repetitive, inward-looking nature, particularly if one practices independently.

The morning shafts of light filtered through the high windows, spotlighting all the airborne dust. Dust on wooden floors makes the surface slippery for felt-soled dance shoes, so Maliyan ran a wet mop over the floor. It became her warm-up. Up and down the floor, she systematically followed the timber lines in time with samba music from her phone. Samba is a party dance, so it has lots of energy. As she didn't like parties, she thought of samba as earthy and tribal, which had the same effect. It worked just as well in getting her body into gear.

MOVE

Although Maliyan enjoyed her solitary practice, she was missing the significant contribution of another person to dance with. She had plenty of self-starting drive to dance by herself, but there was no doubt that another body, another being, another type of energy gave dance a different and wonderful dimension.

> The energy of a healthy, fully functioning male is so different to feminine energy. It pushed her and activated her as a female dancer. His dancing body turned on a switch in her body marked—*MOVE (preferably in time with the music).*

SEDUCTION

We need our men to dance. If we want them to dance, we have to seduce them. But with what?

A young visiting teacher once told Maliyan, "Be sexier. A woman's assets are her hair, boobs, and butt." Maliyan laughed because she thought he was joking. Surely, it was a joke. It wasn't. She looked in the mirror at her hair (no longer than a boy's) and her boobs and butt, which were…ordinary as far as she could tell. She turned towards the teacher and then to his dance partner, who was practising in the far corner of the studio. She was definitely all hair, boobs, and butt—big and luscious. However, she was neither big nor luscious when it came to depth and heart. Although Maliyan understood his focus, she knew that even with ten more years, hair, boobs, and butt would no longer cut it as inspiration. By age thirty, experienced male dancers have seen enough hair, boobs, and butt to last a lifetime. Besides, a significant proportion of male dancers are gay. Female hair, boobs, and butt don't pull much weight.

DIFFERENCE

If we want our men to dance, we have to inspire them. Not with blatant sexuality. That is too common, too little. But with something more, something bigger, something that will give them a reason to want to dance.

The greatest joy of partner dancing is difference. You feed off each other and make the other better and more than we can be on our own. We need difference to help us grow and blossom. It is what happens in life-enhancing relationships. Imagine living with a clone of yourself. How utterly boring. How uninspiring. How intolerable. We need difference to make life worth living. We are drawn to people who change us. Not change us into less of ourselves but into something we cannot be in our own solitary worlds.

BLACKPOOL FEVER

Towards the end of autumn, Maliyan travelled to Geboor, a day's drive from Nanima, at the southern end of the Great Dividing Range. The mountain environment was highly conducive to reflection and spiritual growth. The first important re-coding that came up was about dancing. In late May and early June, a sickness takes over the ballroom dancing world. A magic sort of sickness called Blackpool Fever. It doesn't matter if the dancer has been to Blackpool or not, if they aspire to go or don't, if they religiously watch every livestream or the occasional social media video. Since its inception a century ago, Blackpool Dance Festival has become the most prestigious international ballroom dancing competition of the year.

Champions have fought and been crowned on the hallowed grounds of the Empress Ballroom at the Winter Gardens, Blackpool, England. Fierce battles have been waged in that consecrated space of spectacular architecture. The grand ballroom carries the scars and spoils of war in the air. Once victorious, those revered world champions have been even more fierce in defending their titles. They are the high-heeled, sparkly soldiers, the slicked-hair, perfectly tailored warriors, ticking bodies pitched to perfection with years of intense practice, learning, and finding their unique edge. Those finely-tuned, expensive bodies are driven by concentrated single-mindedness.

The champions forge the way for all dancers—young and old, talented and terrible, rich and poor, gracious and nasty. They blow wind into the sails of countless admiring dancers who reach for their own dancing betterment. Beneath the champions are the troops of dancers who, somehow or other, make the annual pilgrimage to Blackpool despite financial, physical, emotional, and sometimes national difficulties. Each one contributes to the living mass of bodies and souls yearning for the satisfaction of a dance well-danced. A nod from teacher, a mark from respected judge, a smile from partner, applause from a stranger in the audience, a compliment from someone's mother, a glow from inside oneself.

IDOLS

For a spiritual student, idols are both material and nonmaterial forms. They are anything that becomes a God to us. Although we love our dancing, if dancing or anything within it becomes a God to us, we will suffer accordingly.

That does not mean that spiritual seekers should be detached or emotionless. We are highly involved and full of heart, but how we order life in our consciousness differs from others.

> Not to break anyone's dreams, but spiritual seekers are not allowed idols. Not any. None. One by one, they get taken away. Sometimes, it's quick and deadly, but you have to be tough for that. The breaking of idols is not a dream breaker. It is a fear breaker. Getting rid of them is not to create pain. It is to take away pain. The spiritual path doesn't annihilate the source of our happiness. It gives us the possibility of real happiness.

NIL ILL-WILL

Maliyan's love interest, Luna, drove all the way from Nanima to Geboor to visit her (a 12-hour drive). She told him she had found a nearby dance studio, and he asked her about competing again.

> "The thing I love about dancing is dancing," said Maliyan.
>
> She loved her lessons. She loved practising. She didn't like competitions. Ultimately, it is the dancing that all dancers love—to be one with the body, another body, the music, the movement, and the spirit of life. Along the way, that love often gets distorted. But it is still there, waiting to be reignited.
>
> "Competitions turn everyone into competitors," said Maliyan.
>
> "Unsurprising," said Luna.

"Dancers view other dancers as enemies," continued Maliyan. "Teachers eye each other off as threats. Adjudicators compete for pride of place. There are false idols everywhere. However, the thing I like about competing is that you get to share your whole-hearted, best dancing efforts with people who would otherwise never see them. That has nil ill-will."

PART THREE
Dancer Biographies

CHAPTER 19
The Winged Life

He who bends to himself a joy
   Does the winged life destroy;
He who kisses the joy as it flies
   Lives in Eternity's sunrise.

— WILLIAM BLAKE

Some years ago, I did a study on the lives of three well-known dancers/couples from the early to mid-twentieth century. They were all students of Christian Science, which, at that time, was a thriving, innovative, metaphysical, worldwide phenomenon. Following are the resulting articles:

1. Ruth St. Denis
2. Veloz and Yolanda
3. Ginger Rogers

CHAPTER 20
Ruth St. Denis

> We should realize in a vivid and revolutionary sense that we are not in our bodies but our bodies are in us.
>
> — RUTH ST. DENIS

When Ted Shawn first saw Ruth St. Denis perform in 1911, he was enthralled. He was nineteen, a student fresh from religious studies and a ballroom dancer. He looked at the famous, thirty-two-year-old dancer with adoration. She combined his two great loves: dance and spirituality. Little did he realise that, three years later, he would see her again, she would employ him to perform ballroom dancing routines in her shows, and, within the year, they would be married.

Spirituality and dance were the same thing for Ruth. When Ruth was twenty-four in the summer of 1903, she picked up one of her mother's books. It was *Science and Health*, the foundational text of Christian Science by Mary Baker Eddy. Mary was a force to be reckoned with—brave, intelligent, and radical. She was a woman unto Ruth's liking. However, perhaps unlike Mary, Ruth was plagued with personal insecurities that created many emotionally turbulent situations throughout her life.

The first six weeks after reading Science and Health were a turning point of wonderful and beautiful magnitude for young Ruth, and they laid the foundation of her relentless spiritual longing. She said,

> I had never been even dimly aware of the tremendous new world that had now opened before me. All the hours I could spare were spent in reading this book or in going for long walks by myself. I seemed to have joined that class of thinkers who are in the dawn of ideas, eager for a blaze of light. To sense the power of thought as a vast discovery of the soul occupied me for long hours. (I was) filled with wonder and a strange inward vibration which was unlike anything I had ever known before. This definite condition of spiritual ecstasy remained with me for some weeks and then gradually faded, and left as a residue a love of spiritual things and a realization of metaphysical values which has been with me always.
>
> — RUTH ST. DENIS

Ruth always packed the book in her suitcase, along with the Bhagavad Gita and her Ralph Waldo Emerson books, for her trips. She became a lifelong follower of Christian Science and based one of her teaching groups on the book's principles. She applied for formal church membership on two separate occasions but was unfortunately rejected. Even then, the church had the markings of its future downfall—rules and regulations.

DENISHAWN—THE CHILD OF RUTH AND TED'S UNION

> All that is important is this one moment in movement. Make the moment important, vital, and worth living. Do not let it slip away unnoticed and unused.
>
> — MARTHA GRAHAM (STUDENT AND TEACHER AT DENISHAWN BEFORE HER OWN SIGNIFICANT DANCE CAREER).

Denishawn, named after both, was the child of Ruth and Ted's union. It was a performing company, a top dancing school, and a cultural icon of the day. It was a child they nurtured for sixteen years together. Like all good parents, they both played their part. Ruth was the spiritual and aesthetic inspiration. It was she who fascinated audiences (although, later on, Ted became one of the most significant male dancers of his era). Ruth was not good with money and could be emotionally restless and reckless. Ted tended to be more grounded. He maintained the structure and routine of their lives so that their company and school could continue functioning. He was responsible for their financial well-being. After Ted moved away, Ruth had financial problems for the rest of her life. It was an area she could not seem to master. Ted and Ruth were genuine friends. They had a true spiritual, intellectual, and physical compatibility. However, they were also genuine enemies. Both were very ambitious and would often compete with each other with disastrous consequences.

EROTIC, EXOTIC, ESOTERIC

> You and I are but specks of that rhythmic urge which is Brahma, which is Allah, which is God.
>
> — RUTH ST. DENIS

Ruth's free-spirited love of the Divine and, at the same time, honest and uncensored love of the human was the hallmark of her dancing. This combination made for a dynamic, captivating individual. Her dancing was a combination of raw physicality, exotic themes (based mainly on Egypt, India, and Japan), and uplifting and beautiful spiritual treasures of choreography. She was held in awe by her many fans. They were sometimes left speechless after her shows. Some were speechless for other reasons: shock, confusion, indignation, and offence. One of her offences was to dance barefoot. Those close to her loved her with a protective passion. She was a brave dancer.

Ruth and Ted remained married for over fifty years, but the last three decades were spent apart. Both were involved in a range of other relationships, including, for Ted, several gay relationships. They continued to dance with each other, on and off, even into Ruth's eighties. Ruth's relationships tended to be affairs of the heart more than affairs of the body. She longed for emotional and spiritual closeness. She was frequently criticised for her many and varied relationships, often with much younger men. As she possessed a magnetic attractor field for men, it was a rather tempting way for Ruth to try and alleviate her insecurities (with little success, as expected).

Ted told Ruth, much later in their lives, that their

marriage had become an archetypal form of spiritual love to the general population, that it had a special meaning for other people, and that it was not for either of them to destroy that even if they had not lived together for many years. Some wondered if Ted's concern was more for his vulnerable position as a bisexual man in that day and age. For whatever reason, they never did divorce.

CHAPTER 21
Veloz and Yolanda

Frank Veloz and Yolanda Casazza appeared on the cover of the 1939 Time magazine as the *Greatest Dancing Couple*. Both were Christian Scientists at a time when Christian Science was at its height. Yolanda had a natural, humble quietness when she was off-stage. She normally preferred plain day clothes because she said that pretty clothes were for performance. On stage, Yolanda wore delicate and exquisite dresses that Frank designed. She carried a knitted bag with her wherever she went. It contained two books—the Bible and Science and Health. In this way, her faith was always close at hand. Yolanda's strong faith helped her with the usual demands of life and the heavy demands of being constantly in the limelight. The daily reminder of simple, powerful spiritual principles was a protection from the common pitfalls of fame, such as addiction, depression, mental instability, and an ego gone crazy.

Frank and Yolanda's four children were called *the million-dollar babies*. That was how much money each baby cost their parents in lost revenue when Yolanda was pregnant and then attending to a newborn. It was a lot of money in the 1940s. However, money is no protection from life's difficulties, and sadness was no stranger to the Veloz family. Two of the children died in tragic circumstances in their twenties. Also, after several decades of an outstanding partnership, Frank and Yolanda's schools started closing, and their marriage ended. Frank married another dancer, twenty years younger than himself. An entity in her own right, she is still young and dancing today in her mid-nineties. Despite the tides of life, things of beauty and substance remain. Death cannot take away the reality of another's ongoing existence. Divorce cannot annihilate all that is truly good in the forging of a human bond.

When Yolanda and Frank danced, they would prepare themselves for the show by cultivating a genuine sense of love and connection with their audience.

> Frank would walk up and down smoking a cigarette while Yolanda would do a couple of bends to each side. But the real warm-up was psychological. About five minutes before the performance, the area would be cleared so they could concentrate. She would think about dancing with each man, he would think about dancing with each woman in the audience and they revved themselves up with love. When they went on stage this love permeated them and the audience.
>
> — ELIZABETH TALBOT-MARTIN AND WILLIAM TEAFORD

Yolanda was very instinctive when she entered her performing persona on stage. She intuitively and fully gave herself over to that which was much bigger than her normal self. She returned to the other smaller self after performing. Her son, Guy, told me:

> Indeed, my mother did most resoundingly not claim the slightest authorship of what she more or less automatically did. She merely gave herself unto an enigmatic power that was infinitely greater in all matters than any individual ego could hope to master, simply letting IT instead master her.
>
> — GUY VELOZ

Frank and Yolanda, like most dance couples, often fought when practising. Much later, Frank confided to Guy that getting his wife to practice at all was difficult. Nevertheless, when they were performing, all that melted into nothingness.

> It was total co-operation; not competition. Technique was forgotten under a spell of dreamtime.
>
> — GUY VELOZ

Frank told his son that despite the frustrations of practice, he always remained in awe of the spontaneous way Yolanda danced, which complimented his more linear way of thinking. Frank and Yolanda were self-taught dancers, as neither could afford dance lessons when they were younger.

As their show visited different venues, Frank and Yolanda sometimes had to deal with inadequate orchestras. Although Frank would tend to get angry, Yolanda had made an agreement with him that they were to see their orchestras as wonderful. In true Christian Science fashion, choosing to see only the essential, perfect, spiritual nature of all things, she would smile at them with appreciation. Suddenly, and almost miraculously, the less-than-fabulous orchestras would tend to become their much better and more fabulous selves.

Frank, for his part, saw the audience as one breathing entity that was his mission to unite. He would ask the audience if they wished to help out in his and Yolanda's next routine. The orchestra would stop. The audience would then sing, hum, or whistle the melody of songs known to everyone at the time. The lights would be turned down low, and Frank and Yolanda would float majestically to the human-voice orchestra while the hugely enthusiastic audience would be overcome with a feeling of inclusive love.

CHAPTER 22
Ginger Rogers

Fred Astaire's famous dance partner, Ginger Rogers, was a devout Christian Scientist for her whole life. She attended the same branch church as the Veloz's.

The marriage of Ginger's parents ended when she was not much more than a baby. Not long after, young Ginger was kidnapped by her father. At first, Ginger's mother did not know who had taken the child. With the help of a Christian Science practitioner, Ginger was found and returned home. In rather dramatic fashion, her mother travelled to Mexico alone, grabbed the child from her husband's relatives, and, with the assistance of strangers, managed to secretly board a train and return safely to her own home. This was the time before the family law court, equal rights for parents, and strict legal requirements about child custody. After this ordeal, Ginger's mother developed a deep faith in Christian Science and passed it on to her future famous daughter. The two developed a strong bond cemented by early loss.

Later, Ginger's mother married a man named John

Rogers. After healing from a near-fatal illness through his wife's devoted prayer, he also became a Christian Scientist. Ginger said their home was happy, and all three looked in the same spiritual direction, growing together and loving each other.

Ginger was a war bride. Naturally, there was a great need for constant prayer to overcome the debilitating fear of wartime. Ginger would take her young husband to church with her when he was home, and they would try to cope with the tremendous challenges of war as best they could from a spiritual perspective. She wanted them both to stay close to God.

In summarising her life, Ginger spoke heartfully about what was most important to her—her marriages, her mother, and her faith in God. Ginger was married five times. She said she always yearned for a long, happy marriage and loved being married. She enjoyed the security of marriage and was happiest when caring for and loving her mate. She also had a deep appreciation for her mother. Ginger's mother was her rock of stability and the core of unconditional love throughout her highly accomplished life. Above all, Ginger greatly appreciated her religion and the spiritual support and protection it provided her through her long public career.

Of all the many gifts bestowed on me, there is one I treasure above all others–my dear mother. Beyond that, however, is something far greater than success or even family ties–my religion. I owe my health and happiness to it. Without it, I would not have had such wonderful and devoted friends and I couldn't have become the dancer, actress, and person that I am.

— GINGER ROGERS

PART FOUR
Poetry about Dance

CHAPTER 23
Perfect Mismatch

I'm made for ballet,
not latin, but I'm
latin enmeshed.

I'm at home with the ethereal,
not the earth-real, but I'm
latin encaptured.

More aligned with ballet lines.
Fixed spine, moving limbs,
no curves, no face.

In latin, curves are in
and body is out—
out and about on show.

Ballet bodies have neither
sexuality nor individuality.
Closed hips, closed lips.

Latin bodies are as
sensual as they are personal.
Open hips, open lips.

In ballet, one could
disappear into ethereal,
empty-faced egolessness.

Latin keeps you in
body-touching,
hand-searching,

hip-gyrating,
feet-earthing,
centre-rotating,

weight-moving,
face-opening
groundedness.

A constant battle
that cannot be won.
It keeps me here.
A perfect mismatch.

CHAPTER 24
Heart of Existence

If we want our men to dance,
we have to inspire them.
Not with blatant sexuality.
That is too common,
too little.

But with something more,
something bigger,
something that will give them
a reason to want to dance
their life away.

Away, away,
until they have danced
themselves into the
very heart of
existence.

CHAPTER 25
Dissolve

Dance. Don't die.
Edge and push
the body's bondage.
A prisoner reasoning
to cooperate.
Witnessing our isolation.
What could be more alone?

Dance. Don't die.
Together we can escape
the dance we dance alone.
Listen to the rhythmic drum.
The edge is best transgressed
when it is least respected.
Dissolve the separation.

Dance. Don't die.
Bodies touching.
Touching more.
There is not now two.
There is none.
That is the death—
the death of dance.

Dance. Don't die.
Little moments, lost in time,
where edges do not keep us in.
That distant song;
it is so longing for our part.
Dance the dissolve.
Dissolve. Dissolve.

CHAPTER 26
Still Point

The movement is
part of the still.
The still is part
of the movement.

The dancer can be still
and still dance.
They can move
and still be still.

CHAPTER 27
Melded

Glued, but not rigid.
Alive, but not out of control.
Responsive, but not needy.
Melded, but not lost in each other.
Energetic, but contained.
Connected, but independent.
Two become one, move as one.

CHAPTER 28
Grand Old Man

"Dance with me," said
the grand old man.
"I'm strong. I'll lead. I'll wait.
Listen to the music."

The wind moans
its pleasures deep within.
The whip birds call.
Heard, not seen. Whip-whip, tu-tu.

The sun says, "Don't worry."
The river desires nothing.
The wind moans
its joyful pleasures.

"Dance with me," said
the grand old tree.
"Touch my chest
and feel my back.

Become the moaning wind.
You can't bring your body,
but you will have
no need."

CHAPTER 29
Wandering Words

Every move matters.
Movement
talks.

Grand and gentle,
gesture and look
speaks.

Dancers are wandering words,
delicacy and
brutality.

Wandering voiceless words,
body shouting,
body gone.

CHAPTER 30
Burn Up

The challenge of poetry is to convey meaning in very few words. The challenge of dance is to convey life without a single word. The challenge of yoga is to burn up.

> Dancing is my yoga.
> I do it every day.
> Ancient as the Eastern one;
> highway and gateway.
>
> Proper posture.
> Straight spine.
> Lit up, heated up.
> Fire is mine.
>
> Free-flow energy.
> Life-force flow.
> Open the channels,
> activate the glow.

When I'm walking,
I'm rumba-ing along.
Running for the bus,
cha-cha-ing like a song.

Pay attention
or left will trip up right.
Pay attention
or partner will fight.

Spine up.
Step up.
Close up.
Burn up.

Creative Spirit Series

The *Creative Spirit Series* is a 2-book nonfiction series. We don't have desires by accident. Good desires are planted in us because we are meant to follow them, explore them, wrestle with them, and have them form us. If we do this and do it in the right way, the result is happiness. If we do anything in the right way, the result is happiness.

1. The first book of the series is *Dance: A Spiritual Affair*. Dancing is an innately spiritual affair. It is the ever-moving balance between independence and intimacy. This book is written from the perspective of an adult dance student. However, it delves into the emotional and spiritual significance of dance across the board.
2. The second book is *Writing: A Spiritual Voice*. It is about tuning into the writer's spiritual voice and the unique ways our writing develops because of listening and responding to the

Divine. If you are a spiritual seeker and a writer, you will want to use your writing in the same way we use everything to align and expand our spiritual being.

About the Author

2019 DanceSport competition

Donna Goddard shares her love for the Divine and the world with a large international audience and has a strong social media presence. She has authored about twenty books on spirituality and personal growth—nonfiction, fiction, children's fiction, poetry, and specialty books in writing and dance. Her work resonates with people from all walks of life and is a testament to her compassion, empathy, and dedication to helping others. Donna's writing is characterised by warmth, wisdom, and authenticity. She has a gift for connecting with her readers and sharing her insights and experiences in a relatable, accessible, and uplifting way. Donna began her private practice in spiritual healing and counselling in 2005. She lives in rural Victoria, Australia.

All links at https://linktr.ee/donnagoddard

RATINGS AND REVIEWS

Donna would be most grateful for any ratings or reviews.

Also by Donna Goddard

Fiction
Waldmeer Series: A Spiritual Fiction Series
Nanima Series: Spiritual Fiction
Riverland Series (children's fiction 6 to 9 years)
The Fox Tales (children's fiction 8 to 12 years)

Nonfiction
Love and Devotion Series
Spiritual Self Series
Creative Spirit Series
Strange Words: Poems and Prayers
Love's Longing
Master of Me: Meditations

Printed in Great Britain
by Amazon